Classic
Paul Simon

The Simon and Garfunkel Years

A collection of all the music from four landmark Simon and Garfunkel albums.
Arranged for piano/vocal with guitar frames and full lyrics.

Amsco Publications
New York/London/Sydney

Order No. PS 11253
US International Standard Book Number: 0.8256.3311.7
UK International Standard Book Number: 0.7119.2871.1

Exclusive Distributors:
Music Sales Corporation
225 Park Avenue South, New York, NY 10003 USA
Music Sales Limited
8/9 Frith Street, London W1V 5TZ England
Music Sales Pty. Limited
120 Rothschild Street, Rosebery, Sydney, NSW 2018, Australia

Printed in the United States of America by
Vicks Lithograph and Printing Corporation

Sounds Of Silence.

The Sound Of Silence 9
Leaves That Are Green 14
Blessed 18
Kathy's Song 6
Somewhere They Can't Find Me 22
Anji 28
Richard Cory 25
A Most Peculiar Man 34
April Come She Will 42
We've Got A Groovy Thing Goin' 39
I Am A Rock 44

Parsley, Sage, Rosemary and Thyme.

Scarborough Fair/Canticle 48
Patterns 52
Cloudy 58
Homeward Bound 55
The Big Bright Green Pleasure Machine 62
The 59th Street Bridge Song (Feelin' Groovy) 66
The Dangling Conversation 69
Flowers Never Bend With The Rainfall 77
A Simple Desultory Philippic 72
(Or How I Was Robert McNamara'd Into Submission)
For Emily, Whenever I May Find Her 80
A Poem On The Underground Wall 84
7 O'Clock News/Silent Night 88

Bookends.

Bookends Theme 92
Save The Life Of My Child 96
America 102
Overs 110
Old Friends 93
Bookends 114
Fakin' It 116
Punky's Dilemma 122
Mrs. Robinson 130
A Hazy Shade Of Winter 125
At The Zoo 136

Bridge Over Troubled Water.

Bridge Over Troubled Water 142
El Condor Pasa (If I Could) 147
Cecilia 150
Keep The Customer Satisfied 154
So Long, Frank Lloyd Wright 158
The Boxer 166
Baby Driver 163
The Only Living Boy In New York 174
Why Don't You Write Me? 179
Bye Bye Love 184
Song For The Asking 186

Sounds Of Silence.

Kathy's Song

Words and Music by PAUL SIMON

1. I hear the driz - zle of the rain
2. And from the shel - ter of my mind
3. My mind's dis - tract - ed and dif - fused

Like a mem - o - ry it falls
Through the win - dow of my eyes
My thoughts are man - y miles a - way

The Sound Of Silence

Words and Music by PAUL SIMON

Leaves That Are Green

Words and Music by PAUL SIMON

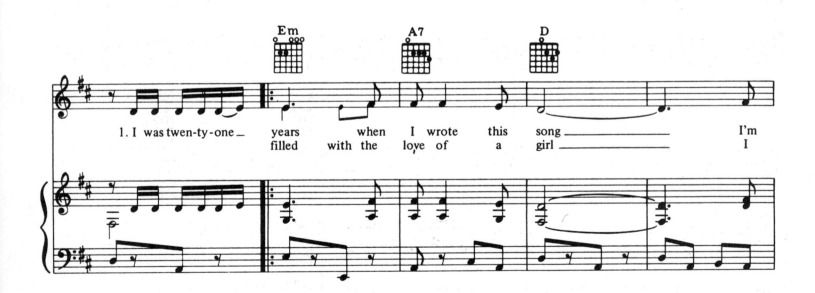

1. I was twen-ty-one years when I wrote this song _____ I'm
filled with the love of a girl _____ I

And they with-er with the wind,_

And they crum-ble in your hand.____ 4. Hel - lo, Hel-

D.S. 𝄋 *al Coda* ⊕

Coda

brown.____

Blessed

Words and Music by PAUL SIMON

Bless - ed   are   the
Bless - ed   is   the
Bless - ed   are   the

meek   for   the   they   shall   in - her -   it.
land   for   and   the   king   -   -   -   dom.
stained   glass,   win -   dow   pane   glass.

Bless - ed   is   the   lamb   whose   blood
Bless - ed   is   the   man   whose   soul
Bless - ed   is   the   church   ser -   vice   makes

Somewhere They Can't Find Me

Words and Music by PAUL SIMON

23

24

Richard Cory

Words and Music by PAUL SIMON

Moderately

Verse:

Dm

C

They say that Rich-ard Cor - y owns one half of this whole town,
pa - pers print his pic - ture al - most ev - 'ry - where he goes;
free - ly gave to char - i - ty, he had the com - mon touch,

Dm

With po - lit - i - cal con - nec - tions to
Rich - ard Cor - y at the op - 'pra, Rich - ard
And they were grate - ful for his pa - tron - age and they

Anji

by DAVY GRAHAM

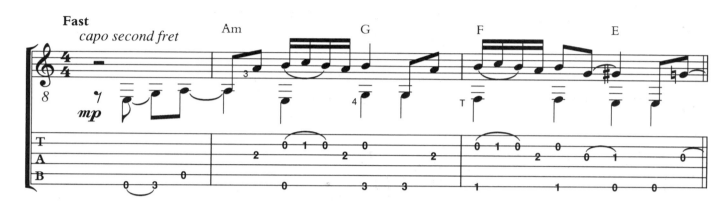

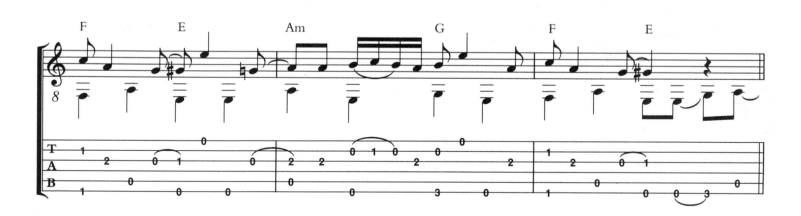

A Most Peculiar Man

Words and Music by PAUL SIMON

We've Got A Groovy Thing Goin'

Words and Music by PAUL SIMON

1. Bad news, bad news! I heard you're pack-in' to leave!
2. wrong, I nev-er hit you when you're
3. know If you're fix-in' to go,

down, I come a-run-nin' right o-ver;
I al-ways gave you good lov-in',
I can't make it with-out you;

April Come She Will

Words and Music by PAUL SIMON

I Am A Rock

Words and Music by PAUL SIMON

Slowly

1. A win-ter's day In a deep and dark De-cem-ber;
2. walls, A fort-ress deep and might-y,
3. love; But I've heard the word be-fore;
4. books And my po-e-try to pro-tect me;

I am a-lone, Gaz-ing from my win-dow
That none may pen-e-trate. I have no need of friend-ship,
It's sleep-ing in my mem-o-ry. I won't dis-turb the slum-ber of
I am shield-ed in my ar-mour, Hid-ing in my room,

Parsley, Sage, Rosemary and Thyme.

Scarborough Fair/Canticle

Arrangement and original counter melody by PAUL SIMON and ARTHUR GARFUNKEL

Are you go - ing _____ to Scar - bor - ough Fair: _____

Pars - ley, sage, rose - mar - y and

bed - clothes the child of the moun - tain.
cleans and po - lish -es a gun.
cause they've long a - go for - got - ten.

work, _____ Then she'll be a true love of
strands, _____ Then she'll be a true love of
heath - er, _____ Then she'll be a true love of

1.2.

Sleeps un - a - ware of the clar - i - on call.

mine. _____
mine. _____

3.

D.S. al Fine 𝄋

mine. _____

Patterns

Words and Music by PAUL SIMON

1. The night sets soft - ly with the hush of fall - ing leaves, _____ Cast - ing
2. (Up a) nar - row flight of stairs in a nar - row lit - tle room, _____ As I
3. (From the) mo - ment of my birth to the in - stant of my death, _____ There are
4. (And the) pat - tern still re - mains on the wall where dark - ness fell, _____ And it's

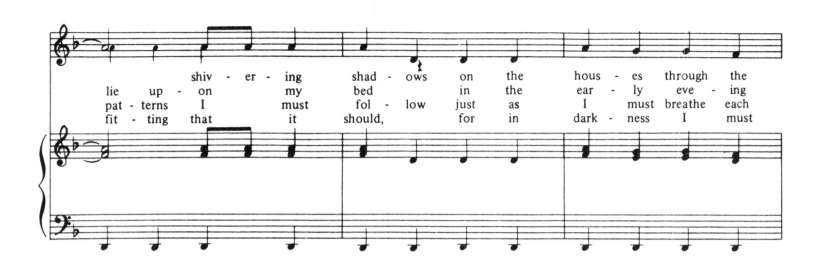

shiv - er - ing shad - ows on the hous - es through the
lie up - on my bed in the ear - ly eve - ing
pat - terns I must fol - low just as I must breathe each
fit - ting that it should, for in dark - ness I must

C

trees, _____ And the
gloom. _____ Im -
breath. _____ Like a
dwell. _____ Like the

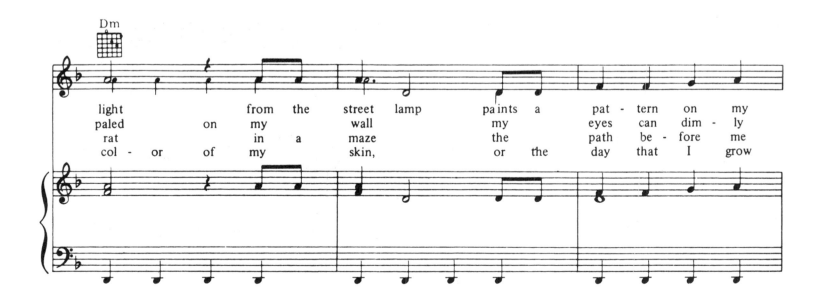

Dm

light from the street lamp paints a pat - tern on my
paled on my wall my eyes can dim - ly
rat in a maze the path be - fore me
col - or of my skin, or the day that I grow

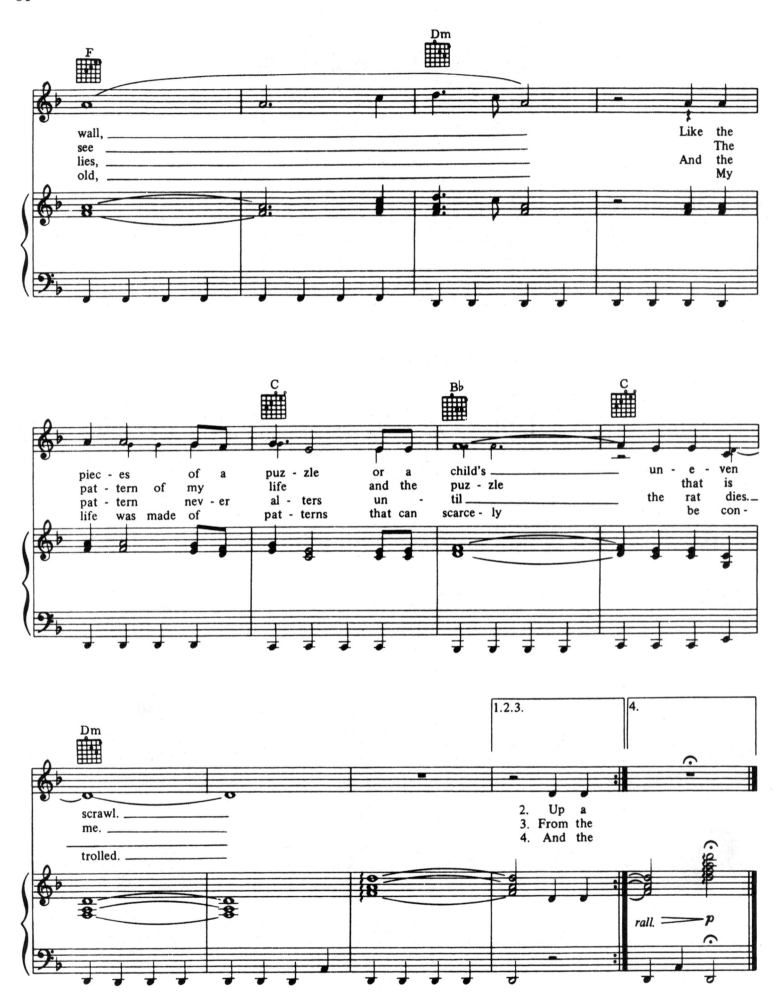

Homeward Bound

Words and Music by PAUL SIMON

1. I'm sit - tin' in the rail - way sta - tion, got a tick - et for my
2. Ev - 'ry day's an end - less stream___ of cig - a - rettes and
(3. To -) night I'll sing my songs a - gain,___ I'll play the game

dest - in - a - tion.___ Mm ___
mag - a - zines.___ Mm ___
and pre - tend.___ Mm ___

Cloudy

Words and Music by PAUL SIMON

The Big Bright Green Pleasure Machine

Words and Music by PAUL SIMON

Well, there's no need to com - plain, ___ We'll e -
Are you wor - ried and dis - tressed? ___ Can't
We can end your dai - ly strife ___ at a

lim - i - nate your pain. ___ We can neu - tral - ize ___ your brain.
seem to get no rest? ___ Put our prod - uct to ___ the test.
rea - son - a - ble price. ___ You've seen it ad - ver - tised ___ in 'Life.'

You'll feel just ___ fine ___ now. ___

Buy a Big Bright ___ Green ___

The 59th Street Bridge Song (Feelin' Groovy)

Words and Music by PAUL SIMON

The Dangling Conversation

Words and Music by PAUL SIMON

1. It's a

| Eb | Bb | F | | Eb | Bb |

still life wa-ter col - or, _____ of a now late af-ter-
read your Em -'ly Dick-in-son, _____ and I my Rob-ert
speak of things that mat - ter, _____ with words that must be

Melody

A Simple Desultory Philippic
(Or How I Was Robert McNamara'd Into Submission)

Words and Music by PAUL SIMON

With a moving beat

I been Nor - man Mai - lered, Max - well Tay - lored.
(I been) Phil Spec - tored, res - ur - rect - ed.

I been John O' - Har - a'd, Mc - Na - mar - a'd.
I been Lou Ad - lered, Bar - ry Sad - lered.

I been Roll - ing Stoned ___ and
Well, I paid all the dues ___

Flowers Never Bend With The Rainfall

Words and Music by PAUL SIMON

Bright tempo

1. Through the cor - ri - dors of sleep Past the sha - dows dark and
2. (The) mir - ror on my walls Past casts an im - age dark and
3. (No) mat - ter if you're born to play the King or

deep ____ My mind ____ dan - ces and leaps ____ in con - fu - sion. ____
small ____ But I'm ____ not sure at all it's my re - flec - tion. ____
pawn For the line is thin - ly drawn 'tween joy and sor - row, ____

For Emily, Whenever I May Find Her

Words and Music by PAUL SIMON

82

A Poem On The Underground Wall

Words and Music by PAUL SIMON

from his pock - et   quick he flash - es,   the cray - on   on the   wall he slash - es,
heart is laugh - ing,   scream - ing, pound - ing,   The   poem a - cross the   tracks re - bound - ing,

Deep up - on the   ad - ver - tis - ing,   a   sin - gle word - ed   poem com - prised   of
Shad - owed by the   ex - it light____   his   legs take their as - cend - ing flight____ to

1.

four   let - ters_____   And his

2.

seek   the breast   of   dark - ness and be   suck - led   by the   night._____

poco rit.

7 O'Clock News/Silent Night

Narration and arrangement by PAUL SIMON and ARTHUR GARFUNKEL
Words and Music by PAUL SIMON

Narration

(Spoken over musical background of "Silent Night")
"This is the early evening edition of the news.
The recent fight in the House of Representatives was over the open
housing section of the Civil Rights Bill.
Brought traditional enemies together but it left the defenders of the
measure without the votes of their strongest supporters.
President Johnson originally proposed an outright ban covering discrimination
by everyone for every type of housing but it had no chance from the start
and everyone in Congress knew it.
A compromise was painfully worked out in the House Judiciary Committee.
In Los Angeles today comedian Lenny Bruce died of what was believed
to be an overdose of narcotics.
Bruce was 42 years old.
Dr. Martin Luther King says he does not intend to cancel plans for
an open housing march Sunday into the Chicago suburb of Cicero.
Cook County Sheriff Richard Ogleby asked King to call off the march and
the police in Cicero said they would ask the National Guard be called
out if it is held.
King now in Atlanta, Georgia plans to return to Chicago Tuesday.
In Chicago Richard Speck, accused murderer of nine student nurses, was
brought before a Grand Jury today for indictment.
The nurses were found stabbed and strangled in their Chicago apartment.
In Washington the atmosphere was tense today as a special sub-committee
of the House Committee on Un-American activities continued its probe into
anti-Viet Nam war protests.
Demonstrators were forcibly evicted from the hearings when they began
chanting anti-war slogans.
Former Vice President Richard Nixon says that unless there is a substantial
increase in the present war effort in Viet Nam, the U.S. should look forward
to five more years of war.
In a speech before the Convention of the Veterans of Foreign Wars
in New York, Nixon also said opposition to the war in this country
is the greatest single weapon working against the U.S.
That's the 7 o'clock edition of the news.
Goodnight."

Bookends.

BOOKENDS / SIMON & GARFUNKEL

Bookends Theme

Words and Music by PAUL SIMON

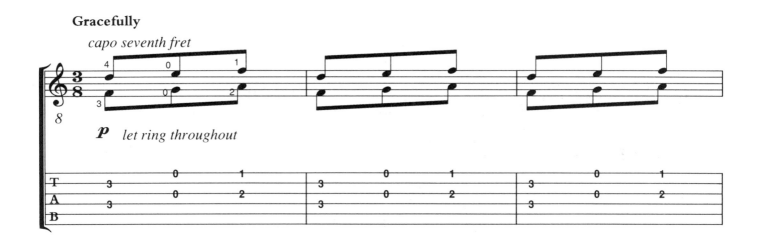

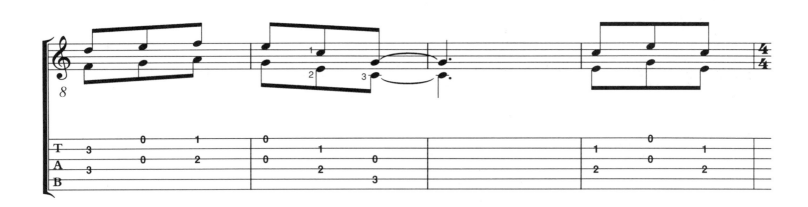

Old Friends

Words and Music by PAUL SIMON

Save The Life Of My Child

Words and Music by PAUL SIMON

America

Words and Music by PAUL SIMON

Overs

Words and Music by PAUL SIMON

Bookends

Words and Music by PAUL SIMON

Fakin' It

Words and Music by PAUL SIMON

120

Punky's Dilemma

Words and Music by PAUL SIMON

A Hazy Shade Of Winter

Words and Music by PAUL SIMON

Moderate tempo

Dm

C

Time, time,___ time,____ See what's be - come of me,_____ while I____

Bb

Am

___ looked a - round for my___ pos - si - bil - i - ties,_____ I was só

Mrs. Robinson

Words and Music by PAUL SIMON

God bless you, please, Mrs. Rob - in - son, Heav - en holds a place

for those who pray, (Hey, hey, hey,

hey, hey, hey.)

Verse:

1. We'd like to know a lit - tle bit a - bout you for our files,

D.S. al Coda

At The Zoo

Words and Music by PAUL SIMON

137

Bridge Over Troubled Water.

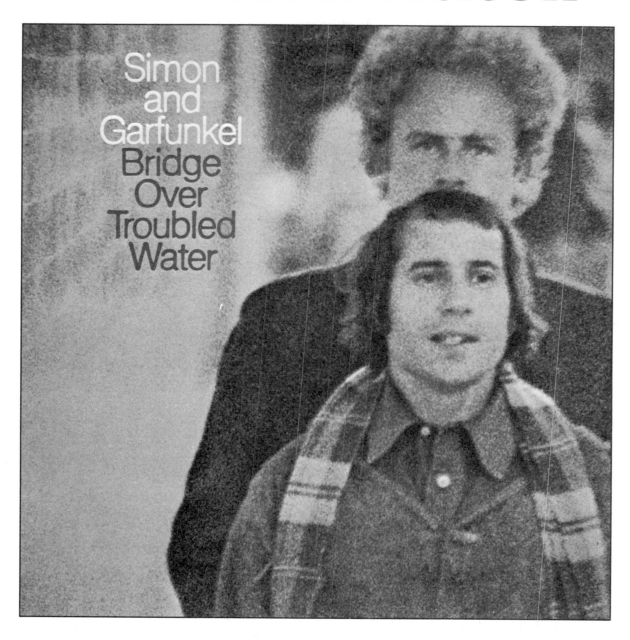

Bridge Over Troubled Water

Words and Music by PAUL SIMON

El Condor Pasa
(If I Could)

English Lyric by PAUL SIMON
Musical arrangement by JORGE MILCHBERG and DANIEL ROBLES

Cecilia

Words and Music by PAUL SIMON

Moderate, not too fast, rhythmically

Cecilia, you're breaking my heart,___ You're shaking my confidence daily.___ Oh, Cecilia, I'm down on my knees,___ I'm

Keep The Customer Satisfied

Words and Music by PAUL SIMON

So Long, Frank Lloyd Wright

Words and Music by PAUL SIMON

Baby Driver

Words and Music by PAUL SIMON

Moderate bright tempo

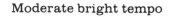

1. My dad-dy was a fam-i-ly bass-man, My ma-
2. (My) dad-dy was a prom-i-nent frog-man, My ma-
3. (My) dad-dy got a big pro-mo-tion, My ma-

ma was an en-gi-neer, ___ And I ___ was born ___ one dark
ma's in the Na-val re-serve, ___ When I ___ was young ___ I car-
ma got a raise in pay, ___ There's no ___ one home, ___ we're all

The Boxer

Words and Music by PAUL SIMON

All lies and jest, still a man hears what he wants to hear, ___ And dis - re - gards the rest. _____

When I left my home and my fam - i - ly, ___ I was

no more than a boy in the com-pa-ny___ of stran-gers in the
qui-et of a rail-way sta-tion run-ning scared, ___
Lay-ing low, seek-ing out the poor-er quar-ters where the
rag-ged peo-ple go, Look-ing for the plac-es on-ly they would

Then I'm lay-ing out my win-ter clothes and wish-ing I was gone, going home

Where the New York Cit-y win-ters are-n't bleed-ing me,

Lead-ing me,

The Only Living Boy In New York

Words and Music by PAUL SIMON

Why Don't You Write Me?

Words and Music by PAUL SIMON

Moderate, with a strong beat

Why Don't You Write___ Me? I'm out_____ in the jun - gle, I'm hun-

- gry to hear___ you.   Send me a card,___ I am wait-

Bye Bye Love

by FELICE BRYANT and BOUDLEAUX BRYANT

CHORUS

Song For The Asking

Words and Music by PAUL SIMON